WOW

Please visit our website at www.twoscoopsicp.com

WOW

Nathan and Patricia Neal

authorHOUSE®

AuthorHouse™
1663 Liberty Drive
Bloomington, IN 47403
www.authorhouse.com
Phone: 1-800-839-8640

Published by AuthorHouse   10/04/2012

ISBN: 978-1-4772-7450-7 (sc)
ISBN: 978-1-4772-7449-1 (e)

Library of Congress Control Number: 2012917916

Table of Contents

PREFACE

As you read popular quotes hopefully you will see
and perhaps understand the choices and systems
created while on our journey. Within the steps we
have taken the quotes will serve as footprints marked
in sands that shouldn't be forgotten by the tides of
time.

For us the "Tide of Time" will not wash away the
memories of the choices and wisdom acquired by the
experiences while starting, opening, and operating
our business.

What's this book about?

- Words of wisdom
- Quotes
- Business /Money
- Life
- Inspiration Messages
- Humor
- Love & Relationships
- Word of Wisdom abc's

This is intended for your entertainment and is in no
way set in stone as to what your personal path will or

will not take you. Remember to be good to yourself and others will follow.

What's in a name? Why wow? W. O. W. = Words of Wisdom . . .

Pat thought since I always seem to use the term WOW to describe or express so many subjects perhaps we could incorporate the expression in our title along with a message. So after much deliberation we agreed on "WOW" or better stated Words of Wisdom! At that moment the birth of this project took on a new path and that is when we experienced a revelation.

WoW Why Not?

Special acknowledgement:

The definition of wow is stated as: <u>expressing astonishment or admiration; natural exclamation.</u>

INTRODUCTION

How many times have you used a phrase heard
in the past by your parents, friends, or significant
others to convey a message. Communication is larger
than merely talking, its words that can symbolically
convey a feeling, message or position you may be
experiencing in life.

This is dedicated to the people who may not know
what to say when in certain situations. This book is
a combination of thought provoking catch phrases
used when my wife and I decided to venture into
starting a new business. The way we communicated
and conveyed our feelings often were expressed in
code.

Several of these codes are catch phrases we will
share with you and hopefully you will have snapshots
of our journey. From conception to completion
was only the start to the realization that starting a
business and running a business is like chalk and
cheese . . . {one of my wife's favorite sayings}.

We had a dream that went from our heads to
paper, to the design phase, architects, back to
design, permitting and licensing, to construction,

production, and then back to our heads. Little did we know the unbelievable "lesson learned" would reveal such impressive victories and memorable trials / tribulations?

For the few who have gone in business for yourselves you may perhaps understand the meaning of the last paragraph and for you who plan or wish to start a business it can't be expressed, explained it must be experienced.

CHAPTER 1

Business and Money

"Our commodity is ice cream and our product is Happiness"

CHAPTER 1

Business / Money

*T*wo broken wheels can not pull a wagon

*T*wo nickels make more noise in a piggy bank than a full piggy bank

*F*ur coat no knickers

*I*f in doubt leave it out

*K*ISS = Keep It Simple Sam

*G*ot to be in it to win it

*Y*ou can't un-ring a bell

*H*ere today and gone tomorrow

*A*ll that glitters
is not gold

No good deed goes un-punished

*E*asy come—Easy go!

*B*elieve half of what you see and less of what you hear

*W*ith the quickness
(Meaning like
yesterday)

*W*e're on the Be—Back—Bus

*B*een there, done that and have the T-shirt!

*W*ould have, could have, should have

Nathan and Patricia Neal

Another day—another dollar

*T*hat person is tighter than Dan's hat band

*W*on't turn anything down but their collar

*P*eople bring People

*P*icture That!

*Y*ou snooze you lose!

*B*ehind the close doors . . .

*T*ake a good look at yourself in the mirror

*T*wo heads are better than one

*I*f it's not broke
don't fix it

*P*ump the brakes

*P*ioneers get slaughtered and settlers prosper

*G*ood help is
hard to find

*L*ook for the MAN with the shiny shoes

*S*ometimes it better
to ask for forgiveness
rather than to await
for permission

*Y*ou only get one
first impression

*O*verhead—vs—Profit hummmm!

*T*hat which does kill you makes you stronger and wiser

CHAPTER 2

Life

"Success is failure turned inside out"

*"When things go wrong, as
they sometimes will,
When the road ahead seems all uphill,
When funds are low, and debts high,
And you want to smile, but have to sigh
When care is pressing you down at bit
Rest if you must but don't you QUIT!*

CHAPTER 2

Life

A closed mouth has never been fed

*I*t's like having a drum with a hole in it, you can't beat it!

*Y*ou have been
beat like a drum

*B*eat with your own stick

Don't throw the baby out with the bath water

*T*he difference is like chalk and cheese

*F*lexibility—strong
as steel yet can
bend like bamboo

Nothing beats a failure but a try

*E*ven a broken clock
is right twice a day

Nathan and Patricia Neal

*O*ne step forward two steps back

A bird in the hand
is better than two
in the bush

A stitch in time
save nine

*D*on't count your
chickens before
they hatch

Sprat to catch
a mackerel

*I*f's and And's—Pots
and Pans this is
not a kitchen

*A*nd's and But's—Candies and Nuts this is not a candy store

*T*houghts are things

*B*e good to yourself

*P*issing on your own boot

*S*low Motion (Don't move to fast)

*Y*ou can't make a
pledge and then flip
the script; you can't
say the words and
not move your lips

*D*on't look a gift horse in the mouth

Nothing comes to a
sleeper but a dream

Nowt as queer as folk

*B*etter safe than sorry

*T*he same faces you meet going up will be the same faces coming down

*H*aste makes Waste

*D*on't get use to being treated bad

*W*hen all else fails kill them with kindness

*T*he grass is not always greener on the other side

*T*he hotter the fire
the stronger the steel

Never judge a book
by it's cover

*Q*ue Sera, Sera
{whatever will
be, will be}

*T*he apple doesn't fall far from the tree

*I*t is what it is!

CHAPTER 3

Humor

"And's and But's
Candies and Nuts
This world is not
a candy store!"

CHAPTER 3

Humor

*U*p the river
without a paddle

*T*hat dog doesn't hunt

*L*eft hand doesn't know what the right is doing

*H*is / Her elevator doesn't go all the way up

*T*he lights are home
yet no one is home

Not the full shilling

*R*aining cats and dogs

*T*hat person is a full glass of water (referring to height)

Stick it where the sun doesn't shine

*F*ish rarely jump
into a boat you
must set the hook

*D*on't worry about the mule going blind just hold on to the line

*T*OO BLOODY RIGHT!

*J*ust because they
call you a dog doesn't
mean you have to
sit up and bark!

Sometimes it's better lucky rather than good

I'm going to whoop somebody's ass (singing)

*W*hat goes around
comes around
"that's why the
world is round"

Check yourself before you wreck yourself

Shut the front door!

*L*et the door knob hit you where the good Lord split you!

*N*ever argue with
a fool—Somebody
watching may
not be able to tell
the difference

*U*p jumped the devil

*T*he beating will continue until morale improves

Dear God, we thank you for our life, health, and strength along with this bounty we are about to receive and Dear Lord please "Do Something"

*I*f you knew better you would do better!

*I*t use to be what
you know, then who
you know, now it's
who knows' you!

*L*et's get the show on the road

*D*on't just talk about it, Be about it!

Nathan and Patricia Neal

*L*ook up, Get up, and Never give up!

So as you think it will be!

Visualize (conceive it, believe it, and achieve it)

*B*e the miracle

Nathan and Patricia Neal

Yes we can—Yes we did!

*I*f you choose not to decide—you still have to make a choice

I think therefore I am

*T*he only thing worse than being talked about is not being talked about

*B*etter to light
a candle than to
curse the darkness
(Chinese proverb)

*Y*ou can't form a line
and not stand alone!

*Y*ou can't pray for hope and crack a joke!

*Y*ou can't say you do,
but then you show
you don't; You can't
say you will and make
sure you won't. *

*T*he mountain doesn't laugh at the river because the river can not stand still, neither does the river laugh at the mountain because the mountain can not move. *

*W*e plan God laughs

CHAPTER 5

Love and Relationships

"Love You More!"
"Laughter needs
no translation"

CHAPTER 5

Love

"God is Love"

*W*hat's good to you is good for you

*L*oving you like a
fat boy loves cake

*L*oving you like
hog loves slop

*Y*ou are like
music to my ear

*Y*ou are the sunshine of my life

*T*oo Hot to handle and too cold to burn

*T*oo right too wrong and too old to learn

*T*wo peas in a pod

*L*ike a hand in a glove

*L*ove you more than yesterday and less than tomorrow

*L*ove you more
(in response to
I love you!)

*L*ike two ships
passing at sea

Relationships

*B*ig I little you!

*B*etter an hour early
than a minute late

.

*T*wo wrongs don't make a right

*D*o unto others as you have them do unto you

*P*ick you friends like
you pick your fruit

*L*aughter is the
shortest distance
between friends

*L*aughter needs no translation

*L*ean on me when
you're not strong

*O*ne good term
deserves another

*Y*our word is your bond

CHAPTER 6

Universal Troubleshooting Guide

Does it work?

CHAPTER 6

Universal
Troubleshooting Guide

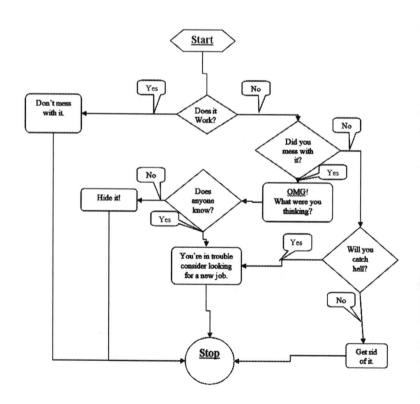

Lesson Learned

What we learned from our journey thus far is the meaning of **KISS** which indeed is so true when going into any business;

K. = Keep **I.** = It **S.** = Simple **S.** = Sam.

As soon as you start thinking to much it will surely cloud your judgment and you're sure to start dropping the balls that were once in the air. Juggling is a learnt skill and as the juggler must constantly practice you must do the same in business also. *Listen twice as much as you speak* perhaps that why we have two ears and one mouth. What we learnt most of all is that everything has its season!

"Give your customers a sense that your business is a special place, created by special people, doing what they should do in the best possible way".

Quoted from Michael E. Gerber book author of "The E Myth"

CHAPTER 7

ABC's

Words of Wisdom

CHAPTER 7

Words of Wisdom

A-Z

*A*pproach each day
with positive thoughts.

*B*elieve in the
goodness of others.

*C*reate a better world
by being a friend.

*D*ecorate your life
with beautiful things.

*E*ducate yourself
through the teaching
of others

*F*ind friendship
through giving
of yourself.

***G**ain insight into others by being a good listener.*

***H**ope will keep dreams alive.*

***I**magination is the key to success.*

*J*udge no one
but yourself.

*K*eep yourself focused
on your goal.

*L*ive life to its fullest.

*M*ake happiness
your primary goal.

*N*othing can stand
in your way when
you dare to dream.

*O*pen your eyes to the world around you.

*P*ersevere when it seems impossible.

*Q*uality of life comes from the things you enjoy.

*R*espect the values
of others.

*S*trive to do your
best in all things

*T*ake hold of your
own destiny.

*U*nity of mind
and soul makes
for inner peace.

*V*alue the little things.

*W*elcome the input
from others.

e*X*plore new opportunities at every chance.

*Y*ou live your life, others will live theirs

*Z*est for life will help you live at your peak.

APPENDIX

During the conception through the completion of the
Two Scoops project their position for experimentation
was a life-line towards success.

There is no such thing as stability either you grow or
decay. Their determination and diversity along with the
assistance of the angels above help bring their dreams to
fruition.

Many blessing have been placed at their table and
perhaps a taste of Nathan and Pat's experiences will be
conveyed in this pocketbook of quotes. Please enjoy the
snapshots and make your own reflections through our
words.

Count your nights by stars not shadows,
Count your days by joy not tears,
And through your lifetime
Count your age by friends not
Years.